101

ESSENTIAL TIPS

Baking

Caroline Bretherton

Produced for DK by
Sands Publishing Solutions
4 Jenner Way, Eccles, Aylesford, Kent ME20 7SQ

Editorial Partners   David & Sylvia Tombesi-Walton
Design Partner   Simon Murrell

Senior Editor   Chauney Dunford
Senior Art Editor   Clare Marshall
Managing Editor   Penny Warren
Jacket Designer   Kathryn Wilding
Senior Pre-production Producer   Tony Phipps
Senior Producer   Ché Creasey
Art Director   Jane Bull
Publisher   Mary Ling

Written by   Caroline Bretherton

First published in Great Britain in 2015 by
Dorling Kindersley Limited, 80 Strand, London WC2R 0RL

A Penguin Random House Company

2 4 6 8 10 9 7 5 3 1

001–266503–May/2015

A CIP catalogue record for this book is available from the British Library.

ISBN 978-0-2410-1469-1

Printed and bound in China by South China Printing Co Ltd

A WORLD OF IDEAS:
SEE ALL THERE IS TO KNOW

www.dk.com

101 ESSENTIAL TIPS

Pages 8 to 17
THE BASICS

Pages 18 to 23
BISCUITS, SLICES & SMALL CAKES

1 ....Read the recipe first
2 ....Room-temperature eggs
3 ....Softened butter
4 ....Butter or baking spread?
5 Toast spices to release the flavours
6 .....Baking soda or baking powder?
7 ....Get the shelves right
8 ....Don't open the oven!
9 ....Oven thermometers
10 ....Baking with chocolate
11 ....Floating test for egg freshness
12 ....Measuring sticky ingredients
13 ....Digital scales
14 ....Unsalted butter for everything
15 ....Using vanilla pods
16 ....Grinding nuts for recipes
17 ....How to slice a cake perfectly
18 ......What if? No greaseproof paper
19 ....What if? No buttermilk
20 ....What if? No baking powder
21 ....What if? No self-raising flour

22 ....Let cookies set
23 ....Perfect brownies
24 ....Achieving even brownness
25 Freezing cookie dough for later use
26 ....Heavy baking trays at hot temperatures
27 ......Using a lumpy mix for muffins
28 A tip for filling cases for cupcakes
29 Using baking spray to ease release
30 ....Remove cupcakes from the tin immediately
31 ....Filling empty tins with water
32 ....A soft top for muffins
33 ....Cutting scones straight down
34 ....Moistening muffins with grated apple or pear

Pages 24 to 27
EVERYDAY & CELEBRATION CAKES

35 ....Tin size
36 ....Greasing & lining tins
37 ....Greasing decorative cake tins
38 ....Letting cakes settle in tins
39 ....Dusting with cocoa for chocolate cakes
40 ....Processing sugar with fruit zest
41 ....Baking with dried fruit
42 ....Using a balloon whisk for dry ingredients
43 ....Double-lining tins for large fruitcakes
44 ....Testing for doneness
45 ......Cutting horizontally for layers
46 ....Storing cakes in the freezer

Pages 28 to 35
FROSTING & FINISHING

47 ....Clean edges
48 ....Preventing icing from picking up crumbs
49 ....Keeping cakes moist
50 ....Improvising a piping bag
51 ....Mixing icing colour
52 ....No time for frosting?
53 ....Quick & interesting toppings for muffins
54 ....Finishing sweet tarts with a blowtorch

55 ....Creating a smooth top layer for frosting
56 ....Finishing frosting smoothly
57 .....Placing decorations in frosting
58 ....Crystallizing edible flower petals for decorating
59 Cheat's crème anglaise for serving

Pages 36 to 45
PATISSERIE, MERINGUES & DESSERTS

60 ....Rubbing butter in
61 ....Using ice-cold water
62 ....Rising overnight in the fridge
63 ....Using butter in Danish pastry
64 ...How to make quick flaky pastry
65 How to make a chewier meringue
66 ....How to clean a bowl for use with egg whites
67 ....How to get whiter meringues
68 ....Avoid cracking
69 ....How to stabilize egg whites
70 ....How to use frozen egg whites
71 ....Removing broken eggshell from batter
72 ....Rolling a Swiss roll or roulade without cracking
73 ....How to prevent a cheesecake from cracking
74 ....How to make a good soufflé

Pages 46 to 55
PIES & TARTS

75 ..How to roll pastry for best results
76 ....How to bind pastry for a richer effect
77 ....How to prevent shrinkage & cracking
78 ....Avoid over-flouring surfaces
79 ....Avoid rerolling
80 ....How to keep pastry crisp when using fillings
81 ....Making hot-water pastry
82 ....How to transfer pastry into a pie tin
83 ....What is blind baking?
84 ....Freezing pastry for later use
85 ....Easy tips for flavouring pastry
86 ....Making attractive pie tops

Pages 56 to 69
BREADS, BATTERS & PIZZAS

87 ....How to start yeast
88 ....Adding salt
89 ....Ambient temperature for rising
90 ....Allowing the dough to rise
91 ....The windowpane test for dough
92 ....Proving before baking
93 ....How to make bagels
94 ....How to make pretzels
95 ....How to give your bread a springy top
96 ....How to achieve a professional crunchy crust
97 ....How to test when bread is done
98 ....Allow to rest before cutting
99 ..Handling & using ciabatta dough
100 .....Handling & using pizza dough
101 ....Making a stuffed-crust pizza

Index 70
Acknowledgments 72

THE BASICS

 ## READ THE RECIPE FIRST

It is easy to get carried away by the baking impulse when you see the tempting image of a luscious cake in a magazine or recipe book. However, it is vital to read a recipe all the way through before you start. The main questions to ask yourself are: "Do I have all the ingredients?" and "Do I have time to make this?"

Read through a recipe before you start

 ## ROOM-TEMPERATURE EGGS

Using room-temperature eggs, even when the recipe does not specifically call for them, is particularly important when you need volume in a cake or dessert. This is because room-temperature eggs can be whisked more easily, resulting in a light, airy texture.

 ## SOFTENED BUTTER

Baking recipes often call for softened or room-temperature butter. When this is the case, take the butter out of the fridge at least 30 minutes before you start baking. Softened butter creams more easily with sugar, creating a light, fluffy texture with little effort.

Take the eggs out of the fridge well in advance

Cut the butter into small squares to soften it

BUTTER OR BAKING SPREAD?

4 Both butter and baking spread have their place in baking – and their advocates. It is not always easy to tell the difference between a cake that has been made with butter and another made with baking spread. Generally speaking, however, butter gives a richer finish to pastry, whereas baking spread will give cakes a lighter, more airy texture.

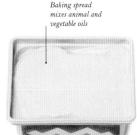

Baking spread mixes animal and vegetable oils

THE SOFT OPTION
One of the advantages of using baking spread over butter is that you do not have to wait until it has softened before working it into the other ingredients.

TOAST SPICES TO RELEASE THE FLAVOURS

5 Using freshly ground spices in a recipe adds a depth of flavour that is hard to beat. If you are using fresh, whole spices, take the time to toast them first. Sprinkle the spices in an even layer in a dry frying pan, and cook them over a low to medium heat for a couple of minutes, or until they start to change colour and release their fragrance. Allow the spices to cool down before grinding them.

KEEP AN EYE ON THE PAN
When you toast the spices, make sure they do not cook too quickly. It they burn, they will produce an unpleasant, acrid flavour.

6 BAKING SODA OR BAKING POWDER?

These two baking staples often get confused. However, they are not the same thing, so it is useful to know which product is most suitable in which circumstances. The main thing to remember is that baking soda needs an acid to activate it, whereas baking powder has already had the acid added to it.

Baking powder is baking soda with added acid, usually cream of tartar

BAKING SODA
Baking soda can be used in any recipe where an acid is present to activate it – most commonly, lemon juice or buttermilk.

BAKING POWDER
Baking powder is typically used in all kinds of baked goods where no other acid is present – for example, vanilla cakes.

7 GET THE SHELVES RIGHT

A good recipe should tell you where to position your oven shelves. Do not overlook this seemingly minor aspect – it is of the utmost importance to the overall success of the bake. Position the shelf before you heat the oven, since hot shelves require careful handling, and time spent juggling them will result in considerable loss of heat.

SHELF POSITION IS IMPORTANT
Moving the oven shelves before you start the bake is not only safer but is more likely to result in the correct oven temperature.

8

DON'T OPEN THE OVEN!

It is tempting, when baking, to take a peek inside the oven to see how things are progressing. However, opening the oven door results in a sudden drop of temperature that can have serious consequences for your bake. A good rule of thumb is never to open the oven door until at least three-quarters of the cooking time allowed for in the recipe has elapsed.

BE PATIENT
Opening the oven too early will result in loss of heat and a slower baking time, and it may cause delicate baked goods to drop.

9

OVEN THERMOMETERS

The temperature dial on your oven may give only an approximate reading. Since the temperature inside the oven is such a vital element of a successful bake, it is worth investing in an accurate oven thermometer. You can leave it in the oven to double-check that the temperature on your dial matches the temperature inside, or use it to check and calibrate the oven's temperature from time to time.

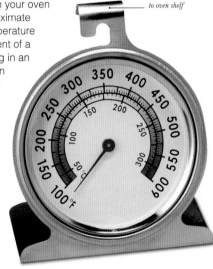

Hook to attach to oven shelf

ACCURATE READING
The loss of heat resulting from opening the oven door takes a few seconds to register. Read the temperature through the glass, if possible.

11

10 BAKING WITH CHOCOLATE

If you are baking with chocolate, it is worth buying the best-quality chocolate you can afford. If you are using dark chocolate, try to find one with a cocoa-solid content of at least 70 per cent. A high cocoa-solid percentage will result in an intense, chocolatey taste rather than a cloyingly sweet one.

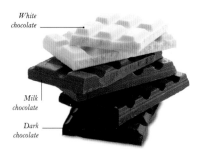

White chocolate

Milk chocolate

Dark chocolate

MELTING CHOCOLATE
A microwave is a good shortcut for melting chocolate, but the higher cocoa-solid content it has, the more likely it is to burn. Instead, melt it in a bain marie – that is, in a glass bowl over a little gently simmering water.

11 FLOATING TEST FOR EGG FRESHNESS

Unless they come with an individual date stamp, sooner or later we all end up with eggs of questionable freshness in the fridge. Before using them in your bake, make sure the eggs are still good to eat by putting them through this simple test.

Floating egg is no longer fresh

Egg that sinks to bottom is fresh

FRESHNESS TEST
Gently place the egg in a glass of cold water to test its freshness. The water must be deep enough for the egg to either sink or float.

12 MEASURING STICKY INGREDIENTS

If your recipe calls for a sticky ingredient such as honey or syrup, measuring can be a messy business. However, there is a trick to ensure that things stay tidy in the kitchen. Simply spray your measuring utensil with a thin layer of baking spray before using (see Tip 29). This will help the ingredients slide off easily.

WARM & STICKY
It is easier to deal with slightly warmed honey or syrup than cold. Before measuring out these ingredients, heat the container under a hot tap for a few seconds.

13 DIGITAL SCALES

Digital scales are an essential piece of equipment for any serious baker. Most have a zeroing, or tare, function, which enables you to measure out several different ingredients into the same bowl. The accuracy of digital scales is such that it is possible to measure out even the smallest amounts.

METRIC OR IMPERIAL?
Good-quality digital scales operate both metric and imperial systems, which eliminates the need to convert grams into ounces and vice versa.

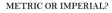

14 UNSALTED BUTTER FOR EVERYTHING

Some recipes may call for both unsalted butter and salt. If you come across this instruction, do not try to save time by using salted butter. Unsalted butter is a better option when it comes to baking, and it is far better to control the amount of salt in the recipe by adding it yourself.

CHOOSING THE RIGHT SALT
Different salts taste differently. Naturally produced flaky sea salt has a delicate, slightly sweet flavour that is complementary to most sweet baked goods.

15 USING VANILLA PODS

Vanilla pods are an expensive, but sometimes essential, luxury when it comes to fine baking. If you do invest in them, it makes sense to maximize their use. After you have scraped out the seeds, the part that is more commonly required in baking, put the empty pods to good use, too.

Vanilla pods

SUGAR STORAGE
After scraping out the seeds, store the pod in a jar of caster sugar to give it a gentle vanilla flavour.

FLAVOURED MILK
To refresh a used vanilla pod, place it in a pan of milk and gently heat it up. Not only will this give the pod a new lease of life, but it will result in delicately flavoured milk.

16 GRINDING NUTS FOR RECIPES

Freshly ground whole nuts yield a more intense nutty flavour than ready-ground ones. Beware of the method you use, though. The best thing to do is to pulse the nuts in a food processor gradually, until you achieve the desired consistency. Grinding them too quickly will release the oils in the nuts, resulting in a greasy paste.

NUTTY CRUMBS
Grinding your own nuts allows you to control the finished texture, making them perfect for decorating either cakes or cupcakes.

GRIND YOUR OWN
Walnuts, hazelnuts, pistachios, macadamia nuts – you can grind all types of nut and use them in baking.

17 HOW TO SLICE A CAKE PERFECTLY

Slicing a frosted cake neatly can be a challenge. For perfect results every time, try the following method. Have a jug of hot water at the ready, and dip your knife into it to heat it slightly. Wipe it dry with a piece of kitchen paper, then slice the cake. Wipe any crumbs off the knife and repeat the process for each slice.

THE PERFECT SLICE
Presentation – of both the entire cake and the individual slices – is important, especially after all the effort you have put into baking it.

WHAT IF?
NO GREASEPROOF PAPER

18

Sometimes a recipe might instruct you to line a baking tin with greaseproof paper. If you do not have any in the house, there is a quick fix. Use good-quality aluminium foil, instead, either lightly sprayed with baking spray or brushed with melted butter or a non-flavoured oil.

Aluminium foil

BETTER CONDUCTOR
Be aware that aluminium foil will heat faster and retain heat better than greaseproof paper. Adjust cooking times accordingly.

Baking spray

WHAT IF?
NO BUTTERMILK

19

Buttermilk is more readily available in some locations than others. If this product should prove hard to find in your local shop or supermarket, it is easy enough to make your own. Simply mix 1 tbsp fresh lemon juice or white vinegar into 250ml (8fl oz) milk. Leave it for a few minutes, until it has curdled and thickened slightly, then use it as you would use buttermilk.

Milk will curdle with addition of acid

ADDING ACIDIC CONTENT
Fresh lemon juice is the simplest addition, but white vinegar or rice wine vinegar can also be used, if you have either to hand.

20 WHAT IF? NO BAKING POWDER

As annoying as it is to realize that you have run out of an important ingredient when you want to bake, it is often possible to improvise an alternative. Such is the case with baking powder. If you find yourself without any in the cupboard, combine ½ tsp cream of tartar with ¼ tsp baking soda. This mix can be used as a substitute for 1 tsp baking powder.

Baking soda and cream of tartar

Baking powder

21 WHAT IF? NO SELF-RAISING FLOUR

If you should find yourself without any self-raising flour, here is a handy substitution: simply whisk together 1 cup (125g/4½oz) plain flour with 1½ tsp baking powder.

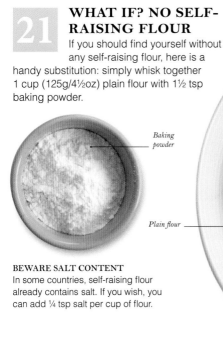

Baking powder

Plain flour

BEWARE SALT CONTENT
In some countries, self-raising flour already contains salt. If you wish, you can add ¼ tsp salt per cup of flour.

BISCUITS, SLICES & SMALL CAKES

22 LET COOKIES SET

It is tempting to eat home-baked cookies the moment they come out of the oven, but it is a better idea to wait. Let them settle on their trays for a couple of minutes before removing them to a wire rack to cool completely. When they are hot, cookies are fragile and can break easily. Plus, if you allow them to cool, you will not burn your mouth when you eat them!

TIME TO REST
Leaving cookies to rest before moving them to a cooling rack allows them to set and makes them less likely to break.

23 PERFECT BROWNIES

Some people enjoy brownies that are very moist in the centre, while others prefer a firmer bake. This difference in consistency depends on the cooking time, so feel free to experiment until you achieve your preferred result.

GOOEY CENTRE
Add 1 tbsp Greek yogurt or sour cream to the mix for an even moister brownie.

24 ACHIEVING EVEN BROWNNESS

Some ovens are hotter on one side than the other. Test the temperature with an oven thermometer (see Tip 9). If you find that this is the case with your oven, you can still ensure a perfectly even brownness on a batch of cookies by rotating the baking sheet halfway through the cooking time.

25 FREEZING COOKIE DOUGH FOR LATER USE

If you like your cookies freshly baked but do not always have time to prepare them, consider making twice as much dough and freezing it. Scoop the extra dough, separated slightly, on to a baking sheet, then open freeze it. Once frozen, transfer the dough portions to a freezer bag. When you need extra cookies, just place them on a baking sheet and bake for a couple of extra minutes, straight from frozen.

HANDY BACKUP
Having a bag of ready-portioned cookie dough in the freezer is very convenient when friends or family drop by unexpectedly.

26 HEAVY BAKING TRAYS AT HOT TEMPERATURES

Good-quality heavy baking trays and tins are essential when baking at high temperatures. A good tray distributes heat uniformly, ensuring an even bake, whereas a cheaper one may brown the outside of a cake before it is cooked through. The same is true with the undersides of cookies and biscuits. In addition, a good-quality tray will not warp in high heat.

PAYING FOR QUALITY
It is well worth investing in good-quality non-stick baking tins – they will produce consistently good results for years to come.

19

27 USING A LUMPY MIX FOR MUFFINS

Muffins are among a small number of baked goods where less beating achieves better results. Muffin batter should be mixed together only until the wet and dry ingredients are just combined. The mixture ought to look a little lumpy. If it is overworked and appears smooth, the muffins will have a dense, rubbery texture.

HAND MIXING IS BEST
Gentle mixing by hand will give you more control over the finished result and make it easier to avoid overmixing.

28 A TIP FOR FILLING CASES FOR CUPCAKES

Cupcakes should be beautifully uniform in size, risen perfectly just above the rims of the papers. To achieve this result, use an ice-cream scoop or large cookie scoop to portion out the batter evenly, and do not fill the papers to the brim. This will also help you avoid dripping the batter on the edges of the papers.

29 USING BAKING SPRAY TO EASE RELEASE

Some cake batters and cookie doughs are sticky and difficult to portion out neatly, even using an ice-cream scoop. Try spraying the scoop lightly with baking spray first. This helps the batter slide out easily in one go. Wipe the scoop with kitchen paper and spray again if needed.

Ice-cream scoop with release

REMOVE CUPCAKES FROM THE TIN IMMEDIATELY

30

It is common practice to let a large cake set in its tin for a few minutes after removing it from the oven. However, smaller cakes, such as cupcakes, can continue to cook if left in a hot tin. For this reason, it is advisable to remove them as soon as possible, taking great care not to burn your fingers. Leave on a wire rack to cool.

EASY REMOVAL
When lifting cupcakes out of a hot tin, gently tug at both sides of the paper at the same time for an even, mess-free removal.

FILLING EMPTY TINS WITH WATER

31

There may be times when, even though you are following a recipe, you might end up not using every space in a 12-hole muffin tin. Before baking, carefully fill the empty spaces half full of water. This will help distribute the heat and allow the other cakes to bake more evenly.

Pour water into empty spaces

WATER WITH CARE
Using a jug with a spout, carefully pour the water until halfway up the sides of the tins before gently sliding the tray into the oven.

A SOFT TOP FOR MUFFINS

32

Muffins bake at quite a high temperature, and it is not uncommon to find that the tops are a little overcooked by the time the inside is done. A simple trick to rectify this is to cover the muffins with a clean, dry tea towel while they cool. The resulting steam will soften the tops slightly, making them perfectly moist.

TEA-TOWEL TRICK
This trick works best with simple muffins; those with a crunchy streusel topping (see Tip 53) should always be left uncovered.

33 CUTTING SCONES STRAIGHT DOWN

When cutting out scones or biscuits, do not be tempted to twist the cutter slightly to release them. This action will cause the edges to bind together, leading to the scones rising unevenly. A straight up-and-down cutting motion is needed for a perfectly risen result.

SHARP METAL CUTTERS
Round metal cutters are preferable to plastic ones, since they give a far sharper result and will last for years.

34 MOISTENING MUFFINS WITH GRATED APPLE OR PEAR

Muffins have a reputation for being delicious straight out of the oven, but they tend to taste dry and stale within only a couple of days. To keep them moister for longer, try adding some grated apple or pear, or even a little mashed banana, to the mix.

ADDED MOISTURE
A single apple, peeled and grated, can be added to almost any muffin mix to produce a moister, longer-lasting muffin.

ADDED TEXTURE
Small pieces of diced fruit added to the mix will give your muffins extra texture, as well as increase their moistness.

EVERYDAY & CELEBRATION CAKES

35
TIN SIZE
Using the correct-sized tin is of the utmost importance when baking. The depth of the batter will impact on a cake's cooking time, so be sure to measure the tins before you start.

Use different tins for different baking purposes

36
GREASING & LINING TINS
To prevent your baked goods from sticking to the bottoms and sides of the tins they are baked in, grease the tins or line them with parchment or greaseproof paper. It is wise to do this even with non-stick tins. This action could save your cake from having to be cut out of the tin in multiple pieces.

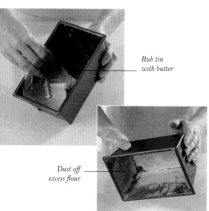

Rub tin with butter

Dust off excess flour

Brush tin with melted butter

Line tin with greaseproof paper

BUTTER & FLOUR
Rub the inside of the tin with butter, then sprinkle it with flour. Allow the flour to reach every corner, then shake off the excess.

BUTTER & PAPER
After brushing the inside of the tin with a little melted butter, line the bottom and sides with cut-to-size greaseproof paper.

37 GREASING DECORATIVE CAKE TINS

The best way to grease decorative cake tins is with baking spray, or with melted butter and a pastry brush, to make sure you get into every corner. Sprinkle the greased tin with a little flour, then tip out any excess for a truly foolproof result.

Get into every groove of tin

Perfect end result

38 LETTING CAKES SETTLE IN TINS

When you take a cake out of the oven, allow it to sit in the tin for at least 10 minutes before turning it out on to a cooling rack to cool completely. The timing is of critical importance: turn the cake out immediately, and it is likely to stick to the tin; leave it too long, and it will become dense.

39 DUSTING WITH COCOA FOR CHOCOLATE CAKES

Dusting a cake tin with flour (see Tip 36) is mostly a good idea, but it does not work well with chocolate cake, since it can lead to a less-than-perfect result, with specks of white flour on the outside. Try dusting the tin with a little unsweetened cocoa powder instead.

40 PROCESSING SUGAR WITH FRUIT ZEST

Citrus zest can be added to most recipes. The best way to maximize the burst of citrussy flavour zest brings is by mixing it in a food processor with the sugar before creaming.

ZESTING TOOLS
Invest in a zesting tool that you can use exclusively for citrus fruit; however, at a pinch, you can use a cheese grater.

BAKING WITH DRIED FRUIT

When baking a fruitcake, the batter should be thick enough to keep the dried fruit from sinking to the bottom. If your batter is not quite right, however, there is a simple trick you can use: lightly toss the dried fruit in a little flour before incorporating it into the batter.

FLOURY COAT
Remove a couple of tablespoons of the weighed flour and use them to lightly coat the dried fruit before mixing it into the batter.

USING A BALLOON WHISK FOR DRY INGREDIENTS

Some recipes call for sifting, a simple procedure that separates any coarse elements in a dry mix, therefore ensuring the lightest possible end result. However, if time is at a premium or if you do not have a sieve, you can produce a similar (and less messy) effect by whisking together dry goods in a large bowl with a balloon whisk.

QUICK & EASY
Whisk together the dry ingredients needed for your baking to replicate a sifting effect.

CUTTING THE RIGHT SHAPE
Take out the bottom of the tin and use it as a template to cut two discs of parchment paper that will fit neatly into the tin.

DOUBLE-LINING TINS FOR LARGE FRUITCAKES

A large fruitcake is a dense thing, and it takes a long time to cook all the way through. This is partly because it must bake at a low temperature to prevent the fruit from burning and losing its sweetness. It is possible to prevent the outside of the cake cooking or over-browning before the inside is set by using a heavy tin and double-lining it with parchment paper.

TESTING FOR DONENESS

Depending on the oven, the time it takes to bake a cake can vary considerably. The main thing to bear in mind is not to check too soon, or the cake will drop. Open the oven only after at least three-quarters of the cooking time have passed. A cake with a cooking time of 25 minutes, for example, can be checked after 20 minutes.

DONE TO THE TOUCH
When a cake is cooked, it should have an even light-brown colour. It should also spring back when gently pressed in the centre.

CHECK THE INSIDE
A metal skewer inserted into the centre of a cake should come out clean, with only a little moisture on it.

CUTTING HORIZONTALLY FOR LAYERS

Cutting a cake horizontally to create the elements for a layer cake can be tricky. The important thing is to get an even result, so take your time.

CAREFULLY DOES IT
Secure the top of the cake with the flat of your hand and cut carefully, rotating the cake as you go.

STORING CAKES IN THE FREEZER

If you are baking ahead, you may need to freeze your cake. For best results, the cake should be frozen as sponges only – no filling or icing. Cool the cake completely, and wrap each piece individually in greaseproof paper followed by several layers of clingfilm, then freeze for up to two months.

FROSTING & FINISHING

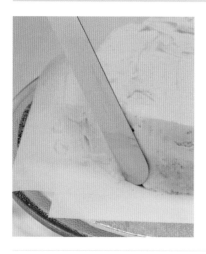

47 CLEAN EDGES

A common mistake made by amateur bakers is to frost and finish a cake, then move it to a serving plate. This inevitably results in the frosting cracking and can ruin a lot of hard work. Frost a cake directly on the serving plate you intend to use to prevent this from happening.

PARCHMENT-PAPER TRICK
Insert strips of parchment paper under the edges of the cake to protect the serving plate as you work. Then slip them out after the frosting is finished.

48 PREVENTING ICING FROM PICKING UP CRUMBS

Decorating a cake takes a little practice, and often crumbs will get into the frosting, affecting the overall neatness of the result. To avoid this, coat the cake with a thin layer of melted and cooled jam, or thinned-out frosting, before applying the final layer of frosting.

QUALITY FINISH
A slightly flexible metal palette knife is an essential piece of equipment for a professionally finished cake.

KEEPING CAKES MOIST

Cupcakes are delicious, but they don't keep well. Because they are so small, they have a tendency to dry out more quickly than larger cakes. To prevent this from happening, be sure to frost them right to the edges of the paper, since this will effectively create an airtight seal around the sponge.

Beautifully frosted cupcakes

SPIRAL FROSTING
For perfect frosting, start around the edges, close to the paper, and spiral around the cake to finish in the centre.

 IMPROVISING A PIPING BAG

Piping bags can be difficult to clean and unwieldy to hold, especially for small quantities of icing. Try improvising your own using a small, strong plastic freezer bag – it's easy to hold for small detail work, and it's disposable, too.

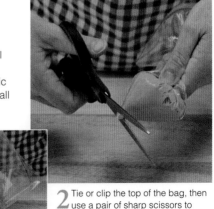

1 Spoon the icing into one corner of the bag, pushing it down gently to avoid air bubbles, which can spoil the finish.

2 Tie or clip the top of the bag, then use a pair of sharp scissors to snip off a small corner. Squeeze the bag gently to release the icing.

MIXING ICING COLOUR

51 Food colouring can transform plain white frosting, turning your cake into a beautifully bright or prettily pale creation. Be aware that a little food colouring goes a long way. For best results, use the tip of a wooden skewer or toothpick to add the colouring a little at a time, until you achieve the desired result.

Bottle of food colouring

VARIED COLOUR PALETTE
To achieve more unusual shades and colours, try combining several colours together, always a little at a time.

Small sieve allows delicate sprinkling

NO TIME FOR FROSTING?

52 Baking can be a time-consuming affair, and sometimes there isn't the opportunity to cool a cake, frost it, and allow the frosting to set before it is served. However, if time is a concern, you can still present a pretty, unfrosted cake. Simply use stencils to add a decorative edge to a fine dusting of icing sugar.

Stencils create shapes

TIME-SAVING DECORATION
Cut your own shapes and use a small sieve or tea strainer to control the amount of icing sugar you sprinkle over the finished cake.

53 QUICK & INTERESTING TOPPINGS FOR MUFFINS

Muffins are some of the simplest, fastest things to bake, and they can contain a wide variety of dried fruits and nuts, as well as other flavourings, either sweet or savoury. Simple toppings, such as a handful of chocolate chunks, a quick streusel topping, or dried banana chips, can add a final flourish to these delicious baked goods.

STREUSEL TOPPING

A streusel topping adds a sweet, crumbly crunch to muffins, cakes, and other baked goods.

A quick streusel topping can be made by rubbing together cold, diced butter, some light soft brown sugar, a handful of oats, and some cinnamon.

This streusel mix stores well in the freezer, in a ziplock bag, and it can be used straight from frozen. Try making a large batch and storing the rest for later use.

Make a large batch and use as needed

54 FINISHING SWEET TARTS WITH A BLOWTORCH

A blowtorch can transform the look of a simple tart in a matter of seconds. Make sure that the tart is chilled before you begin – this will prevent the filling from heating with the flame. Sprinkle a thin layer of very fine sugar over the top of the tart, and use the blowtorch to achieve a brûlée effect.

Flame can be adjusted

CARAMELIZING

Any set custard-like filling can be finished off with a blowtorch and caramelized. Just make sure the tart is well chilled before applying any heat. Leave to set before serving.

55

CREATING A SMOOTH TOP LAYER FOR FROSTING

When making a sandwich sponge cake, instead of creating two layers out of one thick sponge (see Tip 45), which can be quite fiddly, bake two separate sponges. The domed surface of a well-risen cake can be hard to decorate. However, some simple trimming and careful selection can banish any unevenness in minutes, giving your cake the best surface for frosting.

1 Let the sponges rest for at least 5 minutes in their tins; this allows them to set and makes them easier to remove.

2 When the sponges are cool, carefully trim off any uneven surfaces using a large serrated knife and a sawing motion.

3 Apply the filling to the base layer before placing the second sponge in position, choosing the best, flattest side to be the top.

4 A perfectly flat surface will make frosting the cake a simple task and give it a truly professional finish.

FINISHING FROSTING SMOOTHLY

56 The perfect finish to a cake is frosting that has a smooth, even surface. Using a ganache works well here, since this is poured over the cake, and its semi-liquid nature makes it easy to achieve a perfectly smooth finish before it hardens. However, a buttercream frosting can be harder to coax into a smooth finish. A few simple tricks can speed the process along.

1 Dip a large, flexible metal palette knife in hot water. The heat will melt the frosting slightly, smoothing its surface as you work.

2 Wipe the knife quickly to remove any excess water that might spoil the frosting while retaining the heat in the blade.

3 Work around the sides of the cake, rotating it as you go. Use the full extent of the blade to sweep the frosting on the top into a perfectly smooth finish.

57 PLACING DECORATIONS IN FROSTING

Decorating a just-frosted cake can be even harder than frosting one smoothly. A soft ganache may mean the decorations sink in before it hardens; but spend too long frosting, and a simple icing-sugar-and-water frosting can harden before all the decorations are stuck down.

1 To establish how best to arrange the decorations, work it out on the dry, frosted cake first before sticking them down.

2 When you are happy with the overall look, use a small piping bag and a little simple frosting to stick the decorations to the cake.

58 CRYSTALLIZING EDIBLE FLOWER PETALS FOR DECORATING

To add a truly professional flourish to a special-occasion cake, try crystallizing real flowers as decorations. For the best results, source a selection of brightly coloured edible flowers. Make sure they have fairly sturdy petals and that they are not likely to wilt too quickly.

1 Beat together 1 egg white with ½ tsp water, and use this mixture to gently brush the petals all over.

2 Toss some very fine sugar over the petals, and leave the flowers to dry, separated, in a cool, dark place until set.

CHEAT'S CRÈME ANGLAISE FOR SERVING

59 A classic crème anglaise is a simple, stylish sauce that may be served with a rich cake or torte, rather like a thin homemade custard. However, when time is short, try this simple fuss-free alternative, which can be conjured up from just a few basic ingredients.

Single or double cream

Vanilla extract

Icing sugar

QUICK CRÈME ANGLAISE
Whisk together as much cream as you'll need with 1 tbsp icing sugar and ½ tsp vanilla extract to a thick pouring consistency. Transfer to a jug to serve.

Delicious, pourable crème anglaise

PATISSERIE, MERINGUES & DESSERTS

60 RUBBING BUTTER IN

If you wish to make pastry, it is essential that the butter is well chilled before you begin to rub it into the flour. Rubbing butter in by hand takes little effort and is the best way of controlling the end result, since using a food mixer for this task can often result in overprocessing.

1 Use only your fingertips to rub the butter into the flour. This little trick prevents the mixture from overheating.

2 For simple pastry, the finished result should have the texture of coarse breadcrumbs.

61 USING ICE-COLD WATER

Using cold, or even iced, water to bind pastry together is a simple way to achieve better results. Iced water prevents the fats in the pastry from breaking down, which would leave the pastry crumbly and difficult to handle when rolling out.

Jug of chilled water

RISING OVERNIGHT IN THE FRIDGE
Certain baked goods, such as cinnamon rolls, are better served fresh for breakfast, but they are too time-consuming to prepare on the spot. Plan ahead and allow the second rising to happen in the fridge overnight. Just be sure to bring the rolls to room temperature before baking as usual.

Perfectly risen cinnamon rolls

USING BUTTER IN DANISH PASTRY
Most recipes for Danish pastry call for the butter to be rolled out between pieces of greaseproof paper before incorporating it into the dough. However, this is a sticky and time-consuming process. For a simple, fuss-free result, try cutting well-chilled butter into slices and laying them directly on to the pastry.

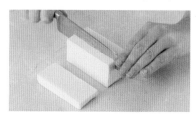

1 Keep the butter in the fridge until it is time to use it to ensure it is well chilled and firm. Cut it into equal-sized slices.

2 Lay the slices of butter evenly on one half of the pastry, making sure you leave a small border all around.

3 Fold the other half of the dough over the butter, pressing the edges together to seal it in.

4 Flour the dough well and roll it out into a rectangle 1cm (⅜in) thick, before folding and chilling it as required.

HOW TO MAKE QUICK FLAKY PASTRY

Making a classic flaky pastry involves a time-consuming process of layering the butter over the dough (see Tip 63), then folding, rolling, and chilling it numerous times for the lightest, flakiest result. Although this traditional method makes a fine pastry, when time is short it is possible to opt for a simple and speedy alternative that produces pleasing results and is also a lot less messy.

1 Put the butter in the freezer for 30 minutes or until it is semi-frozen, to allow it to be grated easily.

2 Gently incorporate the flour into the butter flakes until it is only just combined. This helps retain the texture of the pastry.

HOW TO MAKE A CHEWIER MERINGUE

There are times when a crisp meringue is called for, and others when a chewier result is what is required. To give your meringue a chewier finish, gently fold a teaspoon each of cornflour and white-wine vinegar into the mixture before cooking.

White-wine vinegar

FRESHNESS IS IMPORTANT
Baking staples such as cornflour lose their efficacy if they are old or stale, so check the use-by date.

66 HOW TO CLEAN A BOWL FOR USE WITH EGG WHITES

Whisking egg whites can be a difficult process – even the smallest amount of shell or egg yolk in the bowl can cause the whites to resist your efforts to bring them to soft or stiff peaks. For perfect results every time, go through the following procedure. First of all, ensure that the bowl is perfectly clean, free of any greasy or dusty residue. Next, rub the inside of the bowl with the cut side of a lemon or a little white vinegar, then wipe it dry with kitchen paper before beginning to whisk the egg whites.

CITRUS LAYER
To avoid waste, cut just a little off the end of a lemon – enough that the flesh is exposed – rather than using a whole half.

67 HOW TO GET WHITER MERINGUES

The secret to producing meringues of remarkable snowy whiteness, with a crisp exterior and a hollow interior, is a long, slow cooking time. An extremely low oven heat helps (the ideal temperature being around 120°C/240°F). If your oven doesn't go low enough, consider using a wooden spoon to prop the door open slightly.

DELICIOUS MERINGUES
A meringue is ready when it is crisp on the outside and sounds hollow when tapped gently on the underside.

AVOID CRACKING

Meringues are fragile goods and can crack easily once cooked, which can be very frustrating, since they take so long to bake. Meringues tend to crack because they are susceptible to sudden changes in temperature. Prevent this from occurring by turning off the oven when they are ready and leaving them to cool inside.

COOLING MERINGUES
Once they are cool to the touch, place the meringues on a rack and allow them to cool completely before storing.

 HOW TO STABILIZE EGG WHITES

The more stable the egg-white mixture, the more likely it is to hold its shape and cook into a perfectly crisp, peaked meringue. Although good whisking should achieve this, sometimes a little extra help is needed. Try adding some cream of tartar, white vinegar, or a few drops of lemon juice to the mix after the sugar is incorporated.

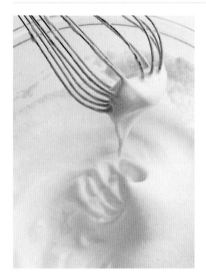

FOLDING IN THE STABILIZER
Be gentle when adding the stabilizing agent into the mix, so as to lose as little volume as possible before baking.

HOW TO USE FROZEN EGG WHITES

If you bake on a regular basis, you will often need the odd egg yolk to bind together a rich pastry. When this is the case, do not throw away the leftover egg white, but freeze it in an airtight container until you have enough to make meringues. There is no need to try to remember how many you have – just defrost them, weigh them, and use double the weight of sugar to egg whites for perfect meringues.

EGG-TO-SUGAR RATIO
Weighing egg whites is a simple trick for calculating the amount of sugar needed for meringues. Use digital scales (see Tip 13) for maximum accuracy.

71 REMOVING BROKEN EGGSHELL FROM BATTER

Every baker knows how annoying it is to crack an egg into cake batter or a bowl only to see a few small pieces of shell appear in the batter, too. It can be remarkably hard to fish bits of eggshell out with a teaspoon or any other kitchen implement. Instead, try using the broken half of the eggshell – the sticky interior of the shell will attract the loose pieces and make them easier to remove.

MINIMIZING SHARDS
Cracking the eggs on a flat surface, such as the counter, rather than the sharp side of a bowl, reduces the likelihood of shards.

72

ROLLING A SWISS ROLL OR ROULADE WITHOUT CRACKING

A roulade is a great dessert for a special occasion or dinner, and it has the added advantage of being easy to transport and serve. To ensure that your roulade makes a good impression on the dinner table, below are a couple of tricks you can use to prevent it from cracking – often the result of an overcooked sponge.

1 When the sponge is ready to come out (see Tip 44), remove it from the oven and invert it on to a clean, damp tea towel while it is still hot.

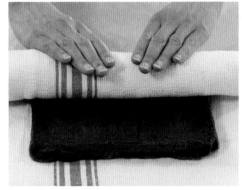

2 Tightly roll the sponge up around the damp tea towel before leaving it to cool. This will help it keep its shape.

PERFECT ROULADE
When the sponge has cooled, carefully unroll it, then fill it and reroll it. If the odd crack appears in the sponge, try disguising it with a decorative flourish.

42

HOW TO PREVENT A CHEESECAKE FROM CRACKING

Rather like meringues, cheesecakes take a long time in a cool oven to cook correctly. Also like meringues, they tend to crack if exposed to quick changes in temperature while they cool. After a lengthy preparation and cooking time, cheesecakes need an equally lengthy cooling time, ideally still inside the oven, to ensure a perfect finish.

1 A cheesecake is done when the surface springs back when gently pressed with a finger and the edges begin to come away from the tin.

2 If you are happy that the cheesecake is baked all the way through, turn off the oven. Do not remove the cheesecake, but allow it to cool inside.

SERVING SUGGESTIONS
Once the cheesecake has cooled and chilled, gently slice it with a sharp knife, and serve it with a fruit coulis or other suitable sauce.

43

HOW TO MAKE A GOOD SOUFFLÉ

Soufflés have a well-deserved reputation for being difficult to make. Every single aspect of the bake – the method, the timing, and even the serving – has to be absolutely correct to produce a perfectly risen dessert. However, with the tips detailed below, making a soufflé can become a fairly straightforward technique to master.

1 A well-greased ramekin, brushed with melted butter, will help the soufflé to rise evenly.

2 Dust the inside of the ramekin with fine sugar, and tap out any excess, to stop the batter from sticking.

3 Cook out the flour in the melted butter. Do this over a low heat to prevent it from browning.

4 Thoroughly whisk the milk into the roux and heat it slowly, stirring to avoid any lumps.

5 Try adding simple flavourings, such as citrus zest, to improve the flavour of a soufflé.

6 When it is time to add the sugar, stir it well to ensure that it has dissolved fully.

7 Wait until the mixture is quite cool before beating in the egg yolks, to prevent them from overheating.

8 Whisk the egg whites well to form medium peaks, so that they will maintain their shape later.

9 When adding the beaten egg whites, start with a single spoon to loosen the mixture.

10 Gently fold in the remaining egg whites, being careful not to lose any volume in the process.

11 Carefully pour the mixture into the centre of the ramekin, filling it up almost to the rim.

12 Rub your finger gently along the inside of the rim to indent the mixture and help it rise straight.

13 When ready, the soufflés should be golden and well risen but still a little molten in the centre. They should be served immediately.

PIES & TARTS

75 HOW TO ROLL PASTRY FOR BEST RESULTS

When working with pastry, the best advice is to keep everything as cool as possible. This includes the environment (the kitchen and the work surface), any tools (from a rolling pin to your hands), and, of course, the pastry itself. Marble boards are ideal for rolling out pastry, since they tend to remain cool.

COOL IS THE WORD
Roll out chilled pastry on a lightly floured surface with a good rolling pin, and apply a gentle pressure to achieve an even surface.

76 HOW TO BIND PASTRY FOR A RICHER EFFECT

Although pastry is commonly made with water, it is also possible to bind it with anything from sour cream to milk for a different effect. Some bakers swear by a teaspoon of vodka to produce perfect pastry.

FOR A RICHER CRUST
An egg yolk beaten with a little cold water can be used to bind the dough together to produce a richer crust.

77 HOW TO PREVENT SHRINKAGE & CRACKING

There are several reasons why pastry shrinks or cracks on cooking, and most concern the overdevelopment of the gluten in the flour. To prevent this from happening, do not overwork your pastry, and always allow it to rest before cooking.

1 Bring the pastry together as quickly as possible, taking care not to handle it excessively.

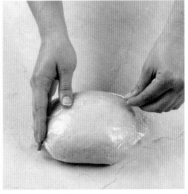

2 Wrap the pastry in clingfilm and chill it for 30 minutes to allow the gluten to relax before rolling it out.

78 AVOID OVER-FLOURING SURFACES

When rolling out pastry, especially a rich, buttery one, it is tempting to keep sprinkling flour on both the pastry and the work surface to prevent it from sticking. However, whenever you do this, you are unintentionally incorporating potentially significant amounts of flour into your delicate pastry. This added flour could change the structure of the pastry, making it hard and dry, so try to be as frugal as possible when flouring the work surface.

A LITTLE GOES A LONG WAY
A good pastry prepared correctly and in a cool kitchen should roll out well without too much added flour.

79 AVOID REROLLING

Rolling out pastry is an acquired skill. As you roll it out, pastry might crack and stick, and in those instances you will have to bring it back together and reroll it. Beware, however, of doing this too often. The additional handling creates heat and activates the gluten in the flour. The resulting pastry could therefore become tough and more liable to shrink on baking.

WASTE NOT
You can put any offcuts of pastry to good use. However, rather than rerolling them into a bigger piece, which is likely to cause the pastry to shrink, try making a few simple tart shells, fill them with jam or lemon curd, and bake them until golden.

80 HOW TO KEEP PASTRY CRISP WHEN USING FILLINGS

Once a pastry case is blind-baked (see Tip 83), it is ready to be trimmed and filled. Placing uncooked fillings, such as cream or crème pâtissière and fresh fruit, directly on the pastry will result in the bottom of the tart case turning soggy. To prevent this from happening, create a protective layer – for example, with jam.

1 While the pastry is still warm, use a small, sharp knife to trim away the excess pastry from the rim of the case.

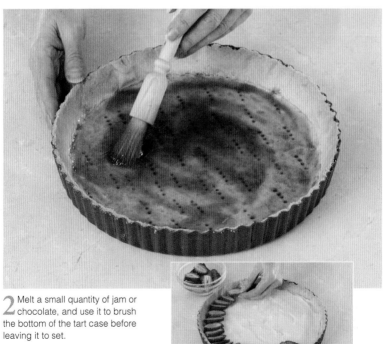

2 Melt a small quantity of jam or chocolate, and use it to brush the bottom of the tart case before leaving it to set.

3 Once the lining is set, fill the tart with your chosen filling, and decorate as required.

MAKING HOT-WATER PASTRY

81 With its use of lard or vegetable shortening, hot-water pastry should be an occasional treat rather than an everyday pastry. Having said that, it is not difficult to prepare, and it produces a gloriously rich, flaky result that is unlike any other kind of pastry. Hot-water pastry is particularly suitable for use with meat products, such as pork and game.

1 Sift the dry ingredients in a large bowl and create a well in the centre.

2 Gently pour the hot melted fat and water into the well.

3 Use a wooden spoon to stir the mixture together until it is well combined.

4 Handling the hot pastry carefully, work to bring it together. You will have to be quite quick, since it will harden as it cools.

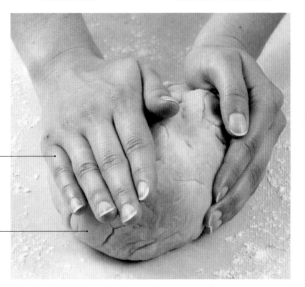

Be careful not to burn your hands

Pastry is easy to work while hot

HOW TO TRANSFER PASTRY INTO A PIE TIN

After you have made and rolled out your pastry, you will have to transfer it from the work surface to a tin. This can be a tricky business, because pastry can break if it is picked up incorrectly. However, the simple method illustrated here will ensure that pastry can be moved quickly and successfully every time.

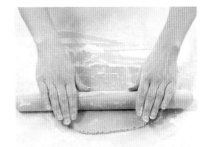

1 Prepare the pastry as usual, rolling it out on a lightly floured work surface to your required thickness.

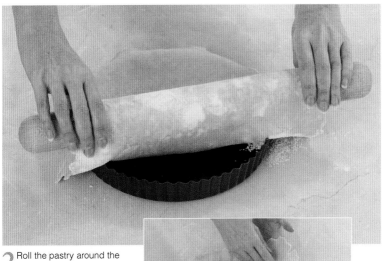

2 Roll the pastry around the rolling pin, then gently unroll it directly over the tin.

3 Press the pastry firmly into the bottom edges of the tin, then up the sides, before trimming off any excess.

83 WHAT IS BLIND BAKING?

Blind baking is a simple, extremely useful method of pre-baking an empty tart case for filling or for storing and using at a later date. The technique is not as difficult as it seems, and it ensures that the bottom of a pie or tart will be cooked through even with the wettest filling. It is possible to purchase ceramic baking beans that can be used over and over; a cheaper alternative is to use dried chickpeas or other pulses, making sure to label them as blind-baking beans when you store them for future use.

1 Prick the bottom of the pastry case with a fork to allow steam to escape. This prevents the pastry rising and forming air bubbles.

2 Line the pastry case with a sheet of parchment paper and fill it with ceramic baking beans or dried chickpeas.

3 Make sure that the baking beans are evenly distributed, covering the bottom of the case in a thick, uniform layer.

4 Once the pastry case is cooked, gently remove the beans and paper. Cook for a further 5 minutes to finish the base.

FREEZING PASTRY FOR LATER USE

Freezing blind-baked pastry cases is a great way to prepare ahead when you have to bake for a large number of people or a special occasion. Bake your pastry cases, wait for them to cool, then wrap them individually in clingfilm, followed by a layer of aluminium foil. Finally, make sure you label them before freezing. The edges of the pastry cases may get knocked and broken if they are piled up or crushed in the freezer, so store them carefully. Even better, freeze individual pastry cases, then stack them in a large container in the freezer.

FREEZE NOW, FILL LATER
It is best to freeze pastry cases unfilled, since the filling can deteriorate in the freezer over time.

FILL WHEN READY TO EAT
Fill the still-frozen pastry cases with the desired filling, and bake them in the usual manner. The baking will refresh the pastry, leaving it as crisp as when it was first cooked.

85

EASY TIPS FOR FLAVOURING PASTRY

Once you have mastered the art of making simple pastry, there are many different twists you can put on it to make it your own. Both sweet and savoury pastry can be flavoured with various herbs and spices to complement the filling. Add just a little to begin with, then bake a small piece of the pastry while the remainder rests in the fridge to see how the flavours work out before you decide whether to add more.

SWEET

A simple addition to any sweet pastry is a couple of tablespoons of caster sugar, which gives a sweet, crisp finish to the pastry. Cocoa can also be added in place of some of the flour.

FLAVOURINGS FOR SAVOURY PASTRY

Fresh herbs such as basil can be whizzed in a food processor with the flour (adding the butter afterwards) to make an attractive summery pastry. A very small sprinkling of thyme, oregano, or sage can be added to a savoury pie or cobbler topping.

Sun-dried tomato paste adds flavour and richness to a Mediterranean tart; or try using your favourite seeds and spices.

Finally, if you're after a pleasing contrast of flavours, try adding grated strong cheddar to an apple pie crust.

SAVOURY

Savoury fillings need only a complementary herb processed into the flour to add colour and flavour to the dish.

86 MAKING ATTRACTIVE PIE TOPS

As key as the taste of a pie is, presentation is also important, and finishing a pie with a decorative design will make it more appealing. There are several techniques that can give your pies the finishing flourish they deserve – from a simple pinch-to-crimp border, to a more elaborate feathering effect. Cut vents in the top to allow any steam to escape.

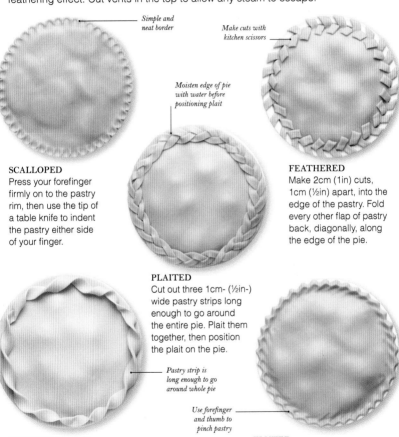

Simple and neat border

Make cuts with kitchen scissors

Moisten edge of pie with water before positioning plait

SCALLOPED
Press your forefinger firmly on to the pastry rim, then use the tip of a table knife to indent the pastry either side of your finger.

FEATHERED
Make 2cm (1in) cuts, 1cm (½in) apart, into the edge of the pastry. Fold every other flap of pastry back, diagonally, along the edge of the pie.

PLAITED
Cut out three 1cm- (½in-) wide pastry strips long enough to go around the entire pie. Plait them together, then position the plait on the pie.

Pastry strip is long enough to go around whole pie

Use forefinger and thumb to pinch pastry

TWISTED RIBBON
Holding a 2cm- (1in-) wide pastry strip at one end, twist it from the other end. Secure it in place.

FLUTED
Pinch the pastry while making indentations at a slight angle in the edge.

BREADS, BATTERS & PIZZAS

 HOW TO START YEAST
Starting yeast to make bread usually involves activating dried yeast with warm water. The temperature of the water is of paramount importance: if it is too cold, the yeast will not activate; but if it is too hot, it will kill the yeast. The ideal temperature of the water is room temperature or lukewarm. A pinch of sugar can help, too.

USING YEAST
Pour the dried yeast (make sure that it is in date) into the warm water, and whisk until it has completely dissolved.

Bubbles and craters on surface of yeast

END RESULT
After a few minutes at room temperature, the mixture should foam up and start to bubble slightly.

ADDING SALT

88 Most breads benefit from the addition of a little salt to enhance their flavour. However, it is important to add the salt at the right time. Adding salt directly to the yeast can kill the yeast and stop the bread rising. To get around this, add the salt to the flour separately to the activated yeast mixture.

MIXING SALT IN
Use a balloon whisk to distribute the salt into the flour evenly before adding the activated yeast mixture.

AMBIENT TEMPERATURE FOR RISING

89 In order for bread dough to rise well and quickly, it needs to be left at the correct temperature. If the temperature is too low, the dough will still rise, albeit very slowly; however, when the environment is too hot, there is the real risk of killing the yeast and stopping the rise altogether. The ideal place for your dough to rise is a warm room, somewhere between 21°C (70°F) and 32°C (90°F). Before leaving the dough to rise, cover it with greased clingfilm.

IDEAL ENVIRONMENT
An oven that has been gently warmed for a few minutes then turned off or an airing cupboard make suitable rising places.

90 ALLOWING THE DOUGH TO RISE

To make sure the dough rises well, put it in a large, clean bowl with plenty of room for it to expand. Spray the inside of the bowl with a little baking spray, then gently place the dough in the bottom. Also spray one side of a large piece of clingfilm, and use it, sprayed side down, to seal the bowl.

SEALING THE BOWL
A warm, draught-free environment will help the dough rise, so make sure the bowl you use is well sealed with clingfilm.

91 THE WINDOWPANE TEST FOR DOUGH

The windowpane test is a simple check that can tell you, at a glance, whether your bread has been kneaded enough and is ready for the next stage. Take a walnut-sized piece of dough and stretch it between the thumbs and forefingers of two hands to make a thin sheet of dough. If the dough is semi-translucent and lets light through it without breaking or tearing, then it is ready to move on.

KNEADING WORKOUT
Use the heel of your hand to push the dough down and away from you to help stretch it out and encourage the necessary elasticity.

LOOKING THROUGH THE DOUGH
To establish whether you have kneaded your dough sufficiently, stretch a small piece of it between your hands. It should not tear.

PROVING BEFORE BAKING

92

After bread has risen for the first time (see Tip 90), it is kneaded briefly (called "knocking back") before being shaped into its final form. It is then left to prove, or rise, for a second time. To help a loaf prove successfully, cover it in greased clingfilm and keep in a warm, draught-free environment, as with the first rise. After proving, the dough may need scoring before baking.

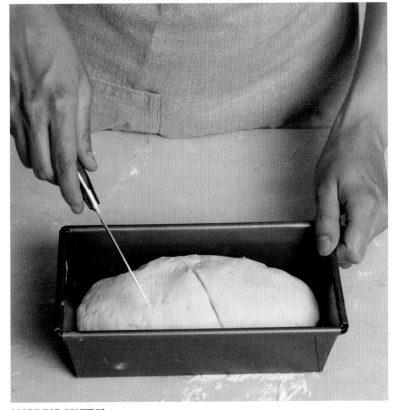

SCORE FOR CONTROL
Scoring a loaf of bread just before baking helps control the direction and height of the rise that will occur in the oven.

HOW TO MAKE BAGELS

93 Bagels are among those baked goods that should be enjoyed as fresh as possible, preferably while they are still warm, right out of the oven. Although professional bagel bakeries have huge steam ovens to help them produce perfect results, the home baker can easily replicate the process at home.

1 Whisk together all the dry ingredients in a large bowl until they are well combined.

2 Add a mixture of activated yeast, water, and a little oil, then bring the dough together.

3 Knead the dough on a lightly floured surface for 10 minutes, until it is stretchy and smooth.

4 Place the dough in a greased bowl in a warm place, and let it rise until doubled in size.

5 Transfer the dough to a lightly floured surface, and divide it into equally sized pieces.

6 Roll each piece of dough gently under the palm of your hand until it forms a fat log shape.

7 Roll and pull each piece of dough until it looks like a fat cigar, about 25cm (10in) long.

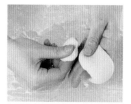

8 Wrap each dough cigar around your knuckles, joining it underneath your palm.

9 Gently squeeze the join together to make a large ring shape, with a large hole.

10 Place the bagels on a lined baking sheet, while you continue to shape the rest of the dough.

11 Cover the bagels with clingfilm greased with baking spray, and leave to rise for a second time.

12 Preheat the oven and at the same time put a large pan of water on the hob to heat.

13 Bring the water to the boil, then turn down the heat and poach each bagel for 1 minute on each side.

14 Remove the bagels from the water with a slotted spoon, and dry them briefly with a clean tea towel.

15 Return the bagels to the baking tray and brush them with a little egg wash.

16 Now the bagels are ready to be put in the oven. Once baked, they should be golden brown, well risen, and glossy to the touch.

Colour is pleasant golden brown

HOW TO MAKE PRETZELS

94

Much like bagels (see Tip 93), pretzels also taste their best the moment they come out of the oven. Although the process for making pretzels is rather lengthy, it is not difficult, and the simple dough needed can be converted into sweet or savoury pretzels, or even wrapped around hot dogs for the ultimate pretzeldog.

1 Whisk the dry ingredients required in a large bowl, and mix them until they are well combined.

2 Sprinkle dried yeast over warm water. Leave it to rest for 5 minutes to activate it.

3 Combine the wet and dry ingredients, and bring them together to form a soft dough.

4 Knead the dough for about 10 minutes, until it is smooth.

5 Place the dough in a lightly greased bowl and let rise in a warm place until it has doubled in size.

6 Turn the dough out on to a lightly floured surface and gently knock it back (knead out excess air).

7 Divide the dough into equally sized pieces and roll them into short, fat log shapes.

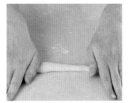

8 Roll the pieces under the palms of your hands, stretching them until they are about 45cm (18in) long.

9 Take each end of the dough and cross them over each other to form a heart shape.

10 Twist the ends of the dough around each other, as though they had linked arms.

11 Secure the ends to the sides of the pretzel – it should still be quite loose.

12 Put the pretzels on a lined baking sheet and cover with clingfilm. Rise them again in a warm place.

13 While the oven is heating, mix ¼ tsp bicarbonate of soda with 2 tbsp boiling water.

14 Brush the risen pretzels with this mixture. It gives them their typical colour and crust.

15 Scatter flakes of sea salt or sesame seeds over the pretzels before putting them in the oven.

16 Five minutes before they are due to come out of the oven, brush the tops with a little egg wash (beaten egg mixed with milk or water) for a final glaze.

17 Once cooked, serve them warm, straight from the oven, with butter, honey, or a little mustard.

95 HOW TO GIVE YOUR BREAD A SPRINGY TOP

Ensure that your bread has a light, springy crust by baking it in a steamy oven. Steam is especially important during the first part of the bake. To introduce steam to the oven, place a roasting tin half full of boiling water in the bottom of the oven just before baking your bread. There are also a few other tricks you can use.

SPRAY THE BREAD
A little water sprayed on to the top of the bread just before cooking should help give it a light, springy crust.

SPRAY THE OVEN
Try spraying the bottom and sides of the oven briefly before you put the bread in, and every ten minutes while it is cooking. Be sure to spray and close the door again quickly, though.

HOW TO ACHIEVE A PROFESSIONAL CRUNCHY CRUST

Next time you buy good-quality bread from a professional bakery, notice its underside, which should have a nice, crunchy crust. Similarly, a good pizza should have a crisp base.

This crunchy finish comes from baking in professional ovens that reach very high temperatures. However, there are a few simple yet effective tricks that can help you achieve these results at home.

PIZZA CRUST

A perfect thin-crust pizza should have a crisp base, as well as being slightly blistered at the edges and puffed up in places. Scatter the baking tray with a little fine cornmeal to help achieve this.

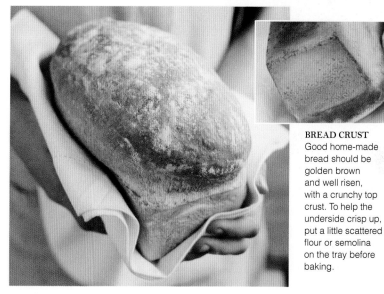

BREAD CRUST

Good home-made bread should be golden brown and well risen, with a crunchy top crust. To help the underside crisp up, put a little scattered flour or semolina on the tray before baking.

97 HOW TO TEST WHEN BREAD IS DONE

To ensure that each loaf is baked to perfection, do not open the oven until at least the minimal cooking time mentioned in your recipe has passed (see Tip 8). At this stage, the most accurate way of determining whether bread is fully baked consists of inserting a thermometer into the centre of the loaf. The temperature should be 94°C (200°F). If you don't have this tool, learn to read the visual and aural signs.

VISUAL INDICATIONS
Bread that is baked to perfection should be golden brown in colour and with a dry, firm crust. It should also detach easily from the baking sheet or tin.

DOES IT SOUND COOKED?
Carefully pick up the bread – use a tea towel to avoid getting burned. Knock on the underside with your knuckles. If it sounds hollow, it means it is ready to come out of the oven.

ALLOW TO REST BEFORE CUTTING

98

It is tempting to cut into home-baked bread as soon as it comes out of the oven and to enjoy a slice while it's still hot. However, if you do so, you will end up with a damp, compressed loaf that will remain misshapen where you've cut it. Allow the bread to rest for at least 20 minutes before you cut into it. This interval will allow the interior steam to disperse gradually, leaving the bread light and springy.

Soft, springy inside

PROFESSIONAL FINISH
Bread that has been allowed to rest is easier to cut into uniform slices and more likely to stay together without crumbling.

99

HANDLING & USING CIABATTTA DOUGH

If you are baking ciabatta bread, make sure that the dough is wet and loose on kneading, since this will help create the large air pockets traditionally found in the finished loaf. Wet doughs are much easier to knead in a machine fitted with a dough hook. If you don't have this particular attachment, however, follow the steps below.

USE YOUR HOOK
When kneading wet dough, a hook prevents the dough from becoming warm and sticky, as it would if you kneaded it by hand.

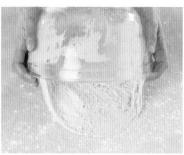

1 Carefully tip the risen dough out of the bowl and on to the work surface, trying to handle it lightly.

2 Knead with your knuckles, trying not to incorporate too much extra flour into the dough, which should remain loose and wet.

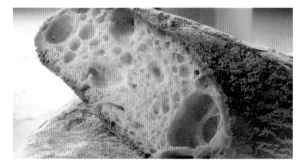

AIR POCKETS
Soft, sticky dough is difficult to handle, but it is the only way to obtain a well-risen ciabatta loaf with the customary large air pockets inside.

100 HANDLING & USING PIZZA DOUGH

Pizza dough is similar to ciabatta dough (see Tip 99), in that it should be a loose, damp dough that is quite delicate to handle. With pizza dough, gentle stretching rather than vigorous rolling is the best way to achieve the desired shape without losing valuable air pockets in the dough.

ROLL IT
Roll the pizza dough out as gently as possible, putting only very little pressure on it.

HANG IT
Use your hands to stretch the dough, and let it hang by its own weight until it gradually grows larger.

STRETCH IT
Finally, use your hands to gently stretch the enlarged dough to its final shape on a lightly floured baking sheet.

101 MAKING A STUFFED-CRUST PIZZA

Once you've mastered the art of baking pizza, you can start experimenting with various toppings and finishes. The heart of the pizza is a good, home-made tomato sauce and fresh mozzarella. After that, anything goes – even a stuffed cheesy crust.

1 If you wish to create a stuffed cheesy crust for your home-made pizza, use shredded mozzarella (not buffalo).

2 Press handfuls of the cheese into thin sausage-like shapes, and place them around the edge of the pizza.

3 Roll the edges of the pizza dough over the cheese, sealing it with a little egg wash, then bake as usual.

INDEX

A B

apples, in muffins 23
bagels 60–61
bain maries 12
baking powder 10, 17
baking soda 10, 17
baking spread 9
baking trays 19
balloon whisks 26
biscuits 18
cutting out 23
blind baking pastry 52
blowtorches, finishing sweet tarts 31
bowls, cleaning 39
bread
ciabatta dough 68
crust 64–5
kneading 58, 68
proving 59
resting before cutting 67
rising 57–8
salt 57
testing for doneness 66
yeast 56
brownies 18
butter 9
in Danish pastry 37
greasing tins 24
quick flaky pastry 38
rubbing in 36
softened butter 8
unsalted butter 14
buttercream frosting 33
buttermilk 16

C

cakes 24–7
cupcakes 20, 21, 29
cutting horizontally 27
frosting 28–30, 32

cakes (continued)
fruitcakes 26
preparing tins 24–5
settling in tins 25
slicing 15
testing for doneness 27
caramelizing 31
cheesecakes, cracking 43
chocolate 12
brownies 18
dusting cakes with cocoa 25
ganache 33, 34
melting 12
ciabatta 68
citrus zest 25
cocoa, dusting cakes with 25
colour, icing 30
cookies 18–19
cooking spray 20
cream of tartar 17, 40
crème anglaise 35
crumbs, icing cakes 28
crust, bread 64–5
crystallizing flowers 34
cupcakes 20, 21, 29
custard 35
cutters 23
cutting cakes horizontally 27

D

Danish pastry 37
decorations
crystallizing flowers 34
in frosting 34
pie tops 55
digital scales 13
doneness, testing for 27, 66

double-lining tins 26
dried fruit 26

E

eggs
frozen whites 41
removing shells from batter 41
soufflés 44–5
stabilizing whites 40
temperature 8
testing for freshness 12
weighing whites 41
whisking whites 39

F

feathered borders 55
flaky pastry 38
flavouring pastry 54
flour
rolling out pastry 48
self-raising flour 17
flowers, crystallizing 34
fluted pastry borders 55
foil, lining tins 16
food colouring 30
freezing
cakes 27
cookie dough 19
egg whites 41
pastry 53
fridges, rising baked goods in 37
frosting 28–30
colour 30
decorations in 34
piping bags 29
smooth top layer for 32
smoothing off 33
spiral frosting 29
fruitcakes 26

G H

ganache 33, 34
greaseproof paper 16
greasing tins 24, 25
grinding nuts 15
honey, measuring 13
hot-water pastry 50

I K

icing see frosting
imperial measurements
    13
ingredients, measuring 13
kneading bread dough
    58, 68

L

layer cakes 27
lemon juice 16, 40
lining tins 16, 24, 26

M N O

measuring ingredients 13
melting chocolate 12
meringues 38–40
metric measurements 13
milk, vanilla 14
muffins
    mixing ingredients 20
    moistening 23
    soft tops 22
    toppings 31
nuts, grinding 15
ovens 10, 11

P

pastry 46–55
    binding 47
    blind baking 52
    crispness 49
    flavouring 54
    freezing 53
    hot-water pastry 50
    ice-cold water 36
    preventing shrinkage 47
    quick flaky pastry 38
    rolling out 46, 48
    rubbing in butter 36
    transferring to pie tin 51

pears, in muffins 23
pie tops 55
pies, pastry 46–55
piping bags 29
pizza 65, 69
plaited pastry decorations
    55
pretzels 62–3
proving bread dough 59

R

recipes 8
ribbon pastry decorations
    55
rising bread 57–8
rolling pastry 46
roulades, rolling out 42
rubbing in butter 36

S

salt 14, 57
savoury pastry 54
scales, digital 13
scalloped borders 55
scones, cutting out 23
self-raising flour 17
shelves, oven 10
sifting ingredients 26
slicing cakes 15
soufflés 44–5
spices, toasting 9
spiral frosting 29
sponges 32, 42
steam, baking bread 64
stencils 30
sticky ingredients,
    measuring 13
storing see freezing
streusel topping 31
stuffed-crust pizza 69
sugar
    finishing sweet tarts with
    blowtorches 31
    processing with citrus zest
    25
    vanilla 14
sweet pastry 54
Swiss rolls 42
syrup, measuring 13

T

tarts
    finishing sweet tarts with
    blowtorches 31
    pastry 46–55
testing for doneness 27, 66
thermometers, oven 11
tins 19
    filling with water 22
    greasing 24, 25
    lining 16, 24
    sizes 24
    transferring pastry to 51
toasting spices 9
toppings, muffins 31
trays 19
twisted ribbon pastry
    decorations 55

U V

unsalted butter 14
vanilla pods 14
vinegar 40

W Y Z

water
    binding pastry 36
    filling empty tins with 22
whisking egg whites 39
whisks 26
windowpane test, bread
    dough 58
yeast 56
zesting tools 25

ACKNOWLEDGMENTS

Sands Publishing Solutions would like to thank
Caroline Bretherton for her efficient and concise writing, as well as for
her assistance in fine-tuning the contents at the outset;
Natalie Godwin for design assistance;
and the ever-brilliant Hilary Bird for making such swift work of the index.

Dorling Kindersley would like to thank the following photographers:
Peter Anderson, Clive Bozzard-Hill, Tony Briscoe, Martin Cameron, Claire Cordier,
Andy Crawford, Peter Gardner, Steve Gorton, Will Heap, Ruth Jenkinson, Dave King,
David Munns, David Murray, Simon Murrell, Ian O'Leary, Gary Ombler, William Reavell,
Matthew Richardson, Charles Schiller, Howard Shooter, Clive Streeter, Carole Tuff,
Kate Whitaker.